D1563450

Books by Philip Levine

Poetry

Unselected Poems   *1997*
The Simple Truth   *1994*
What Work Is   *1991*
New Selected Poems   *1991*
A Walk with Tom Jefferson   *1988*
Sweet Will   *1985*
Selected Poems   *1984*
One for the Rose   *1981*
7 Years from Somewhere   *1979*
Ashes: Poems New and Old   *1979*
The Names of the Lost   *1976*
1933   *1974*
They Feed They Lion   *1972*
Red Dust   *1971*
Pili's Wall   *1971*
Not This Pig   *1968*
On the Edge   *1963*

Essays

The Bread of Time   *1994*

Translations

Off the Map: Selected Poems of Gloria Fuertes,
edited and translated with Ada Long   *1984*
Tarumba: The Selected Poems of Jaime Sabines,
edited and translated with Ernesto Trejo   *1979*

Interviews

Don't Ask   *1981*

Unselected Poems

UNSELECTED POEMS

Philip Levine

Greenhouse Review Press

Acknowledgments

Some of the poems in this volume were originally published in the following journals: "The Letters" was originally published in *Boulevard;* "This World" was originally published in *Georgia Review;* "Going Back," was originally published in *Gettysburg Review;* "Keep Talking" was originally published in *Poetry;* "Ascension," "Another Song," and "On the Language of Dust" were originally published in *The New Yorker;* "The Harbor at Nevermind" was originally published in *Southern Indiana Review.*

Poems from the following previously published books are included in this volume: NOT THIS PIG, copyright 1963, 1964, 1965, 1966, 1967, 1968 by Philip Levine; published by Wesleyan University Press. RED DUST, copyright 1971 by Philip Levine; published by Kayak. THEY FEED THEY LION, copyright 1968, 1969, 1970, 1971, 1972 by Philip Levine; published by Atheneum. 1933, copyright 1972, 1973, 1974 by Philip Levine; published by Atheneum. THE NAMES OF THE LOST, copyright 1976 by Philip Levine; published in a limited edition by The Windhover Press of The University of Iowa, and in a trade edition by Atheneum. ASHES, copyright 1971, 1979 by Philip Levine; published by Atheneum and in a limited edition by Graywolf Press. SEVEN YEARS FROM SOMEWHERE, copyright 1979 by Philip Levine; published by Atheneum. ONE FOR THE ROSE, copyright 1981 by Philip Levine; published by Atheneum. SWEET WILL, copyright 1985 by Philip Levine; published by Atheneum.

The press would like to thank Christopher Buckley, Mark Ferrer, and Jon Veinberg for their assistance with the production of this book.

GREENHOUSE REVIEW PRESS
3965 Bonny Doon Road
Santa Cruz, California 95060

ISBN 0-9655239-0-X
Manufactured in the United States of America
First Edition

For Les Bluesteins

Hands I have taken, face I have kiss'd, mortal I have ever touch'd, it shall be you.

Table of Contents

Four

Introduction

Almost fifty years ago I journeyed to New York City from my native Detroit to hear Dylan Thomas read at the 92nd Street Y. I was at the time convinced he was the greatest living poet, and knowing his reputation as a boozer I thought it best to seize the day. I enjoyed his patter between the poems almost as much as the poems, and one of his asides has stayed with me all of my life. He was speaking of sending out his poems to seek their fortunes in the world; some brought back large checks in the mail and others came back, he said, "with their tails between their legs." At the time my poetry had received only a single letter of rejection, but that was because I'd attempted publication only a single time. It was of some comfort to know that even as great a poet as Thomas still experienced grief, but even more exciting was the thought that one could consider the poem as a creature on its own once loosed from its maker. Over the years I've come to think of my poems in that manner. Some years later my oldest son once asked me seriously—he could be a startlingly serious boy for such a funloving person—, "Pop, how many poems do you think you have out there working for you?" Like Thomas's aside my son Mark's statement made a profound impression on me. Because of my working days in Detroit and the poetry that came out of it, I like to think of myself as a "worker," but according to my son I was an employer, and when I thought about it seriously it was clear that while I worked at poetry, and it could be impossibly difficult work at which I often failed, I was also unlike most workers completely in possession of the means of production. I controlled the fate of those little workers, the poems, I had created.

In 1984 when I decided to put together a selected poems, I had no idea I was condemning many of the creatures of my own making to obscurity, for at that time only a single book of my authorship, my first book, *On the Edge,* was out of print or contained poems largely unavailable to an interested reader. (My third book, *Red Dust,* was also out of print, but I'd included in *Ashes* all the poems from it I still thought worthy.) My editor at Atheneum, which was then my publisher, was Harry Ford, who was and still is, I am convinced, the finest poetry editor in the country, and when he gave advice I listened. Harry and I did not agree on the size and scope of my selected poems. I envisioned a book similar to my favorite little collections of poetry: the selection Rexroth did of the poems of D.H. Lawrence, Jarrell's *William Carlos Williams, One Hundred and Seventy Chinese Poems* translated by Arthur Waley in a little Cape paperback, the Penguin Zbigniew Herbert, books I'd been toting with me for years whenever I got a job outside Fresno. These were small books carved out of enormous collections of what I regarded as great poetry; I could carry one in my jacket pocket and read it at the bus stop or on the bus. I thought my own book might be no more than a hundred pages, something a student or lover of poetry might stick in his or her pocket or backpack and carry for comfort or diversion or pleasure through the cities of the world. Harry wanted a book of considerable heft and range; he wanted—certainly for my sake—to make his author look as significant as possible.

At that time I also sought the advice of several close friends. I asked them to list those poems they thought absolutely essential for such a collection. At the time I thought all but one failed me; they gave me comparable and huge lists that included very few poems from my earliest books and almost all of the poems from the more recent ones. I wondered if they weren't merely telling me what I wanted to hear: that as a poet I was getting better and better with age. (I was once told by a fellow poet who I'd observed sleeping through my reading that my new poems were fantastic.

I hadn't read any new poems.) Only my wife took my request with absolute seriousness: she gave me a list of the dozen poems she thought had to be included. I thought she might have stretched it to twenty.

Harry and I compromised, and I gave him a book of eighty poems, one almost twice as long as those compact books that had meant so much to me. Although readers complained to me that I'd left out their favorite poems, I was pleased with the book and the three good reviews it got. A few years later Harry was relieved of his duties at Atheneum, and one by one the eight books of mine they'd published went out of print, for there was no one there who gave a fig for poetry. Those poems, with the exception of the ones included in my *New Selected Poems,* have remained out of print and until the publication of this book all of them were unavailable to new readers of my work unless they had access to a good library or an exceptional used book store.

I know perfectly well my readers can get along without those poems not included in my *New Selected Poems,* those heretofore unselected poems. It is the poems themselves I am concerned with, shut off from the eyes of readers, no longer doing anything for anyone. I want them to be fulfilled and useful; hence the present volume, which is made up of those poems I now believe are the best of those left in the dark. Since 1984 I have published four new collections, but only one—*Sweet Will,* my last with Atheneum before the company died the death it deserved for firing Harry—is out of print; I have added poems from it for this book. Since the most recent three (all with Knopf and edited by Harry) are still in print I've taken nothing from them; instead I've opted for a small selection of poems that for one reason or another I chose not to include in those books and now wish

I had. Until this book they too were unselected. I never meant to injure or insult any of my poems; it has always seemed to me that they've done far more for me than I've done for them. I am pleased with this opportunity to undo the harm I did to them. I can only hope those I've chosen enjoy their hour in the light and work like mad.

Philip Levine

One

Coming Homeward from Toledo

We stopped at a beer garden,
drank, and watched the usual farmers
watching us, and gave a dull
country laborer a lift
in the wrong direction. He
giggled by the roadside where
we left him, pissing in snow
and waving, forty frozen
miles from home.

                When the engine
failed, we stood in a circle
of our breathing listening for
the sounds of snow.

             Later
just before the dawn of the
second day of a new year
already old, we found her
under white heaps, another
city in another time,
and fell asleep, and wakened
alone and disappointed
in a glass house under a
bare wood roof.

            I called out for
you, my brothers and friends, and
someone's children came, someone's
wife—puzzled helpful faces—
saying "father" and "husband."
You never answered, never

heard, under the frozen stars
of that old year where the snow
creaked in great mounds and the air
bronzed from the slag heaps twenty
miles south of Ecorse, for you were
happy, tired, and never going home.

Commanding Elephants

Lonnie said before this, "I'm
the chief of the elephants.
I call the tunes and they dance."
From his bed he'd hear the drum

of hooves in the bricked alley
and the blast of the Sheenie
calling for rags, wood, paper,
glass—all that was left over—

and from this he'd tell the time.
Beside the bed on a chair
the clean work pants, on the door
the ironed work shirt with his name,

and in the bathroom farther
than he could go the high-top
lace-up boots, the kind the scouts
wore and he'd worn since

he was twelve. To be asleep
hours after dawn, to have
a daughter in school when he
woke, a wife in the same shop

where he'd been the foreman
and said Go, where he'd tripped
the columns of switches and
brought the slow elephant feet

of the presses sliding down
in grooves as they must still do
effortlessly for someone.
"Oh my body, what have you

done to me?" he never said.
His hands surprised him; smelling
of soap, they lay at his sides
as though they were listening.

House of Silence

The winter sun, golden and tired,
settles on the irregular army
of bottles. Outside the trucks
jostle toward the open road,
outside it's Saturday afternoon,
and young women in black pass by
arm in arm. This bar
is the house of silence, and we drink
to silence without raising our voices
in the old way. We drink to doors
that don't open, to the four walls
that close their eyes, hands that run,
fingers that count change, toes
that add up to ten. Suspended
as we are between our business
and our rest, we feel the sudden peace
of wine and the agony of stale bread.
Columbus sailed from here 30 years ago
and never wrote home. On Saturdays
like this the phone still rings for him.

Where We Live Now

1

We live here because the houses
are clean, the lawns run
right to the street

and the streets run away.
No one walks here.
No one wakens at night or dies.

The cars sit open-eyed
in the driveways.
The lights are on all day.

2

At home forever, she has removed
her long foreign names
that stained her face like hair.

She smiles at you, and you think
tears will start from the corners
of her mouth. Such a look

of tenderness, you look away.
She's your sister. Quietly she says,
You're a shit, I'll get you for it.

3

Money's the same, he says.
He brings it home in white slabs
that smell like soap.

Throws them down
on the table as though
he didn't care.

The children hear
and come in from play glowing
like honey and so hungry.

4
With it all we have
such a talent for laughing.
We can laugh at anything.

And we forget no one.
She listens to Mother
on the phone, and he remembers

the exact phrasing of a child's sorrows,
the oaths taken by bear and tiger
never to forgive.

5
On Sunday we're having a party.
The children are taken away
in a black Dodge, their faces erased

from the mirrors. Outside a scum
is forming on the afternoon.
A car parks but no one gets out.

Brother is loading the fridge.
Sister is polishing and spraying herself.
Today we're having a party.

6
For fun we talk about you.
Everything's better for being said.
That's a rule.

This is going to be some long night, she says.
How could you? How could you?
For the love of Mother, he says.

There will be no dawn
until the laughing stops. Even the pines
are burning in the dark.

7
Why do you love me? he says.
Because. Because.
You're best to me, she purrs.

In the kitchen, in the closets,
behind the doors, above the toilets,
the calendars are eating it up.

One blackened one watches you
like another window. Why
are you listening? it says.

8
No one says, There's a war.
No one says, Children are burning.
No one says, Bizniz as usual.

But you have to take it all back.
You have to hunt through your socks
and dirty underwear

and crush each word. If you're serious
you have to sit in the corner
and eat ten new dollars. Eat 'em.

9
Whose rifles are brooding
in the closet? What are
the bolts whispering

back and forth? And the pyramids
of ammunition, so many
hungry mouths to feed.

When you hide in bed
the revolver under the pillow
smiles and shows its teeth.

10
On the last night the children
waken from the same dream
of leaves burning.

Two girls in the dark
knowing there are no wolves
or bad men in the room.

Only electricity on the loose,
the television screaming at itself,
the dishwasher tearing its heart out.

11
We're going away. The house
is too warm. We disconnect
the telephone.

Bones, cans, broken dolls, bronzed shoes,
ground down to face powder. Burn
the toilet paper collected in the basement.

Take back the bottles.
The back stairs are raining glass.
Cancel the milk.

12
You may go now, says Cupboard.
I won't talk,
says Clock.

Your bag is black and waiting.
How can you leave your house?
The stove hunches its shoulders,

the kitchen table stares at the sky.
You're heaving yourself out in the snow
groping toward the front door.

Alone

Sunset, and the olive grove flames
on the far hill. We descend
into the lunging shadows
of goat grass, and the air

deepens like smoke.
You were behind me, but when I turned
there was the wrangling of crows
and the long grass rising in the wind

and the swelling tips of grain
turning to water under a black sky.
All around me the thousand
small denials of the day

rose like insects to the flaming
of an old truth, someone alone
following a broken trail of stones
toward the deep and starless river.

The Cutting Edge

Even the spring water
couldn't numb the slash
of that green rock
covered with river lace.
Slowly the blood spread
from under the flap of skin
that winked open; deep in
my foot, for a second, I saw
something holding back,
and I sat down in the water
up to my waist in water,
my pockets filling with it.
I squeezed the green rock,
pressed it to my cheeks,
to my eyelids. I did not
want to be sick or faint
with children looking on,
so I held to the edge of the stone
until I came back.

That was a year ago.
I threw the stone away
as though I could banish it
from creation; I threw
it into the dry reeds,
where it could do no harm,
and dragged myself bleeding
up the hillside and drove home.

I forgot the stone
drying among burned reeds
in October; I forgot

how cold this place got
when the winds came down the pass,
and how, after the late rains,
the first pale ice-plants dot
the slopes like embroidery,
then larkspur, myrtle, and the great,
bellowing, horned blooms
that bring summer on.

Huddling to where it fell,
like a stunned animal,
the stone stayed. I kneel
to it and see how dust
has caked over half of it
like a protruding lip
or a scab on no cut
but on a cutting edge.
It comes away from the ground
easily, and the dry dirt
crumbles, and it's the same.
In the river its colors
darken and divide
as though stained; the green
patterning I thought lace
is its own, and the oily shine
comes back, and the sudden smell
of dizziness and sweat.

I could take it home
and plant it in a box;
I could talk about
what it did to me
and what I did to it,

or how in its element
it lives like you or me.
But it stops me, here
on my open hand,
by being a stone, and I send
it flying over the heads
of the fishing children,
arching alone above
the dialogue of reeds,
falling and falling toward water,
somewhere in water to strike
a conversation of stone.

The Way Down

On the way down
blue lupine at the roadside,
red bud scattered
down the mountain, tiny
white jump-ups hiding
underfoot, the first push
of wild oats like froth
at the field's edge. The wind blows
through everything, the crowned
peaks above us, the soft floor
of the valley below,
the humps of rock
walking down the world.

On the way down
from the trackless snow fields
where a blackbird
eyed me from
a solitary pine, knowing
I would go back the way
I came, shaking my head,
and the blue glitter of ice
was like the darkness
of winter nights, deepening
before it could change,
and the only voice
my own saying
Goodbye.

Can you hear me?
the air says. I hold
my breath and listen

and a finger of dirt thaws,
a river drains
from a snow drop
and rages down
my cheeks, our father
the wind hums
a prayer through my mouth
and answers in the oat,
and now the tight rows of seed
bow to the earth
and hold on and hold on.

Waking in Alicante

Driven all day over bad roads
    from Barcelona, down
      the coast. The heat

murderous, the air clogged with dust,
    to arrive at evening
      in Alicante, city

of dim workers' quarters, bad trucks,
    furious little bars
      and the same heat.

I awaken at 4, tasting fried calamares
    and the salty beer the sea
      has given us,

tasting the bitterness of all the lives
    around me in the darkness
      fumbling toward dawn.

My smallest son, on the same narrow
    bed, his knees pumping
      sporadically

as though he ran into the blackness
    of sleep away from all
      that sleep is not—

the dark creased women that hover
    above each soiled turnip,
      each stained onion,

that bleed the bread sour with their thumbs,
  the old beaten soldiers in ruined
    suits, dying

in the corners of bus stations, talking
  in bars to no one, making
    the night roads

to nowhere, and the long gray-legged boys
  hiding their tears
    behind cupped hands.

How much anger and shame falls slowly
  like rain into his life
    to nurture

the strange root that is the heart
  of a boy growing
    to manhood.

It grows in the shape I give it
  each day, a man,
    a poet

in middle age still wandering in search
  of that boy's dream
    of a single self

formed of all the warring selves split
  off at my birth
    and set spinning.

The slate hills rising from the sea,
  the workers' fortress I saw
    bathed in dust,

the rifle loops crumbling like dead mouths,
  the little promontory
    where the deaths

were done thirty years ago, the death
  still hanging in the burning
    air, are mine.

Now I have come home to Spain, home
  to my Spanish self
    for this one night.

The bats still circle the streetlight
  outside my window
    until the first

gray sifting of dawn startles their eyes
  and the motorcycles start
    up, rocketing

down the high narrow streets.
  Teddy stirs next
    to me, a life

awakening once again to all the lives
  raging in the streets,
    and to his own.

Who will he be today, this child
  of mine, this fair
    and final child?

The eyes dart under soft lids
  and open and the world
    once more

is with him, and he smiles at me,
  the father welcoming
    him home.

Ruth

They would waken
face to face, the windshield
crystaled, the car
so cold they had to get out.
Beyond the apple orchard
they saw where the dawn sun
fell among plowed fields
in little mounds of shadow
and a small stream ran black below
where the rocks slept.
Her wrists pounding
against it, she rubbed
the water into eyes
and temples, the iron taste
faint on her tongue.
And they'd get going, stopping
for cokes and gas
and cold candy bars all
through Ohio,
and when the sun failed
north of Toledo
they were almost there,
the night sky burning
up ahead at River Rouge
like another day.

Another day.
Now he was gone, the children
grown up and gone
and she back home,
or whatever you could call it,
West Virginia.

A wafer of sunlight
on the pillow, and she rose
and heard the mice startled
beneath the floorboards. Washed
in the sink, lit the stove,
and waited. Another day
falling into the fields, tufted
like a child's quilt.
Beyond the empty yard
a wall of poplars stared back,
their far sides
still darkness, and beyond,
its teeth dulled with rust,
the harrow tilted
on one frozen wheel, sliding
back to earth.

Two

For the Fallen

In the old graveyard behind
the fortress of Montjuich
side by side are buried
the brothers Ascaso and
Buenaventura Durruti.
If you go there and stand
in the June sun or under
the scudding clouds
of November you will
hear neither the great wail
of the factories or the sea
groaning into the harbor
laden with goods and freckled
with oil. You will hear
the distant waves of traffic
in the late afternoon rush
and maybe the yellowed grass
eating, for this is that
time in Barcelona, you
will hear your own breath
slowing and time slowing
and then the death of time
because it stops here. You
can go down on your knees
and pray that the spirit
of men and women come back
and inhabit this failing flesh
but if you listen well
your heart will ask
you to stand, under
the fading sun or
the rising moon, it

doesn't matter, either
alone or breathing as you
do now the words
of the fallen and the slow
clouds of diesel exhaust.
Look at your hands. They
are not scarred by
the cigarettes of the police,
and the palms are soft,
the fingers long but
slightly kinked, the hands
once of a boy stained
with the ink of dull reports
the day they laid
Buenaventura beside Francisco
Ascaso and thousands gathered
weeping or somber. The nails
were bitten down then.
The comrades must have known
it was over, and Joaquín
Ascaso, staring at the earth
that had opened so quickly
for his brothers, must
have whispered *soon*.
Soon the boy rose
from his desk and went
into the darkness
congealing in cold parlours
or in the weariness
of old pistons, in the gasps
of men and women asleep
and dreaming as the bus
stalls and starts on the way

home from work. And Joaquín,
who had never knelt, rose
and went home to prepare,
knowing he was all
of them, as you know
they are all that gathers
in your hands, all
that is left, words
spoken to no one
left, blurred in
the waves of the old sea,
garlands of red roses
that tattered, chips
of light and dark, fire
and smoke, the burning
and the cold that were
life and can still
shiver these two stiff
and darkening hands.

Elegy for Teddy Holmes, Dead In a Far Land

1
Here the air takes the host
of the air, rain tipped with ether
and a wafer of smoke.
It is August and you are gone
two years into the earth.
Near the cold source the streams
thicken with froth, the hawk—
who is your laughter—
wakens, his wings glued
to the high cedar branch.

If she were alive, my Aunt Tsipie
would say a prayer against your going
(you were so much alike
with your dark heads of patience,
your large hands,
and the smiles pinched at the end).
She would hold your book
unopened, and nod that she knew
nothing of such things,
and go on dressing the child,
who in middle age can't count her fingers.
All the playmates went off
and sent back tall ugly strangers
and some like you sent no one.

2
Your wife writes us about the end,
she doesn't say how the larks
fled down the lanes
of the broken grove,
she doesn't say how the table

sighed under her palms
when she begged to hold you
and was denied,
she doesn't say how she walked
out alone after dinner
past the open windows
where the girls sewed and mended,
past the station of closed shutters
where the cop dozed in a green cape,
how she heard the chant of the seashell,
the muttering of chalk,
how where water was black
and each drop burned
she pledged in this odd tongue
and was frightened.

3
Our fathers gone forever and apart
into the lies of the city,
our mothers stunned in the schoolrooms
before the sudden blood of men and boys,
the eyes of animals, the skin
of girls burning like raw opal,
how clearly you saw it all.

And at the end you saw the earth tip
and barns and trees and old rusted trucks
slide away,
the fields peel away,
and then the dry clay
underneath us all, the drawn brow
of an old woman, tired
of being called each night
to bring wine to the grown ones,
water to the young.

The Falling Sky

Last night while I slept
someone woke and went
to the window to see
if the moon was dreaming
in the October night.
I heard her leave the bed,
heard the floor creak
and opened my eyes a moment
to see her standing in all
the glory living gives us.
I caught a scent of lilacs,
and thought, but that was
years ago, and slept again.

Today, I want to ask her
what she hoped to find
last night, I want to say,
I'm with you in this life,
but Nikolai, her boyish
eucalyptus, bucks in the wind,
the long grasses that hold
the seeds of the harvests
to come, give as they must,
and she is busy tying down
and piling dead grass on.

Nothing I can say will stop
the great bellied clouds
riding low over the fences
and flat wooden houses
of this old neighborhood

or keep the late roses
from shredding down to dust.

The first drop splatters
on the back of my hand,
then the second. Time
to go in, says the wind,
and I do. From the window
blurring before my poor eyes,
I see her growing smaller,
darker, under the falling sky.

For the Poets of Chile

Today I called for you,
my death, like a cup
of creamy milk I
could drink in the cold dawn,
I called you to come
down soon. I woke up
thinking of the thousands
in the *futbol* stadium
of Santiago de Chile,
and I went cold, shaking
my head as though
I could shake it away.
I thought of the men
and women who sang
the songs of their people
for the last time, I
thought of the precise
architecture of a man's wrist
ground down to powder.
That night when I fell asleep
in my study, the false
deaths and the real blurred
in my dreams. I called
out to die, and calling
woke myself to the empty
beer can, the cup
of ashes, my children
gone in their cars,
the radio still moaning.
A year passes, two,
and still someone must
stand at the window

as the night takes hold
remembering how once
there were the voices
of play rising
from the street,
and a man or woman
came home from work
humming a little tune
the way a child does
as he muses over
his lessons. Someone
must remember it over
and over, must bring
it all home and rinse
each crushed cell
in the waters of our lives
the way a god would.
Victor, who died
on the third day—
his song of outrage
unfinished—and was strung
up as an example to all,
Victor left a child,
a little girl
who must waken each day
before her mother
beside her, and dress
herself in the clothes
laid out the night
before. The house sleeps
except for her, the floors
and cupboards cry out
like dreamers. She goes

to the table and sets out
two forks, two spoons, two knives,
white linen napkins gone
gray at the edges,
the bare plates,
and the tall glasses
for the milk they must
drink each morning.

Any Night

Look, the eucalyptus, the Atlas pine,
the yellowing ash, all the trees
are gone, and I was older than
all of them. I am older than the moon,
than the stars that fill my plate,
than the unseen planets that huddle
together here at the end of a year
no one wanted. A year more than a year,
in which the sparrows learned
to fly backwards into eternity.
Their brothers and sisters saw this
and refuse to build nests. Before
the week is over they will all
have gone, and the chorus of love
that filled my yard and spilled
into my kitchen each evening
will be gone. I will have to learn
to sing in the voices of pure joy
and pure pain. I will have to forget
my name, my childhood, the years
under the cold dominion of the clock
so that this voice, torn and cracked,
can reach the low hills that shielded
the orange trees once. I will stand
on the back porch as the cold
drifts in, and sing, not for joy,
not for love, not even to be heard.
I will sing so that the darkness
can take hold and whatever
is left, the fallen fruit, the last
leaf, the puzzled squirrel, the child
far from home, lost, will believe

this could be any night. That boy,
walking alone, thinking of nothing
or reciting his favorite names
to the moon and stars, let him
find the home he left this morning,
let him hear a prayer out
of the raging mouth of the wind.
Let him repeat that prayer,
the prayer that night follows day,
that life follows death, that in time
we find our lives. Don't let him see
all that has gone. Let him love
the darkness. Look, he's running
and singing too. He could be happy.

A Woman Waking

She wakens early remembering
her father rising in the dark
lighting the stove with a match
scraped on the floor. Then measuring
water for coffee, and later the smell
coming through. She would hear
him drying spoons, dropping
them one by one in the drawer.
Then he was on the stairs
going for the milk. So soon
he would be at her door
to wake her gently, he thought,
with a hand at her nape, shaking
to and fro, smelling of gasoline
and whispering. Then he left.
Now she shakes her head, shakes
him away and will not rise.
There is fog at the window
and thickening the high branches
of the sycamores. She thinks
of her own kitchen, the dishwasher
yawning open, the dripping carton
left on the counter. Her boys
have gone off steaming like sheep.
Were they here last night?
Where do they live? she wonders,
with whom? Are they home?
In her yard the young plum tree,
barely taller than she, drops
its first yellow leaf. She listens
and hears nothing. If she rose
and walked barefoot on the wood floor

no one would come to lead her
back to bed or give her
a glass of water. If she
boiled an egg it would darken
before her eyes. The sky tires
and turns away without a word.
The pillow beside hers is cold,
the old odor of soap is there.
Her hands are cold. What time is it?

Montjuich

"Hill of Jews," says one,
 named for a cemetery
 long gone. "Hill of Jove,"
 says another, and maybe
 Jove stalked here
 once or rests now
 where so many lie
 who felt God swell
 the earth and burn
 along the edges
 of their breath.
 Almost seventy years
 since a troop of cavalry
 jingled up the silent road,
 dismounted, and loaded
 their rifles to deliver
 the fusillade into
 the small, soft body
 of Ferrer, who would
 not beg God's help.
 Later, two carpenters
 came, carrying his pine
 coffin on their heads,
 two men out of movies
 not yet made, and near dark
 the body was unchained
 and fell a last time
 onto the stones.
 Four soldiers carried
 the box, sweating
 and resting by turns,
 to where the fresh hole

waited, and the world
went back to sleep.
The sea, still dark
as a blind eye,
grumbles at dusk,
the air deepens and a chill
suddenly runs along
my back. I have come
foolishly bearing red roses
for all those whose blood
spotted the cold floors
of these cells. If I
could give a measure
of my own for each
endless moment of pain,
well, what good
would that do? You
are asleep, brothers
and sisters, and maybe
that was all the God
of this old hill could
give you. It wasn't
he who filled your
lungs with the power
to raise your voices
against stone, steel,
animal, against
the pain exploding
in your own skulls,
against the unbreakable
walls of the State.
No, not he. That
was the gift only

the dying could hand
from one of you
to the other, a gift
like these roses I fling
off into the night.
You chose no God

but each other, head,
belly, groin, heart, you
chose the lonely road
back down these hills
empty handed, breath
steaming in the cold
March night or worse,
the wrong roads
that lead to black earth
and the broken seed
of your body. The sea
spreads below, still
as dark and heavy
as oil. As I
descend step by step
a wind picks up and hums
through the low trees
along the way, like
the heavens' last groan
or a song being born.

Songs

Dawn coming in over the fields
of darkness takes me by surprise
and I look up from my solitary road
pleased not to be alone, the birds
now choiring from the orange groves
huddling to the low hills. But sorry
that this night has ended, a night
in which you spoke of how little love
we seemed to have known and all of it
going from one of us to the other.
You could tell the words took me
by surprise, as they often will, and you
grew shy and held me away for a while,
your eyes enormous in the darkness,
almost as large as your hunger
to see and be seen over and over.

30 years ago I heard a woman sing
of the motherless child sometimes
she felt like. In a white dress
this black woman with a gardenia
in her hair leaned on the piano
and stared out into the breathing darkness
of unknown men and women needing
her songs. There were those among
us who cried, those who rejoiced
that she was back before us for a time,
a time not to be much longer, for
the voice was going and the habits
slowly becoming all there was of her.

And I believe that night she cared
for the purity of the songs and not
much else. Oh, she still saw
the slow gathering of that red dusk
that hovered over her cities, and no
doubt dawns like this one caught
her on the roads from job to job,
but the words she'd lived by were
drained of mystery as this sky
is now, and there was no more "Easy
Living" and she was "Miss Brown" to
no one and no one was her "Lover Man."
The only songs that mattered were wordless
like those rising in confusion from
the trees or wind-songs that waken
the grass that slept a century, that
waken me to how far we've come.

Asking

Once, in the beginning
on the last Sunday
of a lost August,
I sat on the Canadian shore
of Lake Huron and watched
the dark clouds go over,
knowing this was the end
of summer. There was a girl
beside me, but we
barely knew each other,
and so we sat
in our separate thoughts,
or I did anyway. I saw
how it would be, summer
after summer, working
toward a few days like this
when I came flushed
with strength and money,
my hands scarred
and hardened, my shoulders
and arms thick, and maybe
I would find a girl
or maybe I'd get drunk
and fight or growing older
just get drunk and sit
alone staring into a glass
the way my uncles did.
When I felt the girl's hand
on the back of my neck
I shuddered the way you do
when a cool wind
passes over you, and she

misunderstood and pulled
her hand away. I took
her hand in mine and said
something about having
drifted off and how odd
it was to know a season
had ended at one moment
and I had turned
toward winter, maybe
a lifetime of winters.
Then I thought of her
working week after week
in the office
of a small contractor
she said she hated
and going home to the father
she said she hated
and the mother who went on
about marriage and was
she ever going to get out,
and she just barely 22.
Almost 30 years ago.
She and I never saw
each other after we
got back to Detroit
in the smoky light
of early evening.
I let her out
a block from her house
and said I'd call her,
but knew I wouldn't
knowing what I did
about her life and how

she needed someone
I wasn't. I went back
to my room and sat
in the dark wondering
how can I get out.
I knew there must be
millions of us,
alone and frightened,
feeling the sudden chill
of winter, of time
gathering and falling
like a shadow across
our lives. Wondering
what was the answer.
Only a boy, still alone,
still solemn, turning
in the darkness
toward manhood, turning
as the years turned
imperceptibly, petal
by petal, closing
for the night,
the question still
unanswered, that question
never to be asked again.

Salt

This one woman has been sobbing
for hours. The last plane has gone,
and no one is left except the porter
mopping the floors and an old woman
cleaning out the ash trays and wiping
the chrome handles of the chairs.
No one has asked her to leave because
there are no more flights and even the cop
down the tiled hall has fallen asleep.
The plane has by now entered the night
somewhere between Chicago and Cleveland,
and below the lights of cities are going
on and off or perhaps there are cloud banks
or perhaps the man in the window seat
is blinking his eyes. Soon they will
pass over water. No one will think,
Thus did the Angel of Death before he
descended upon Egypt only to find
the Egyptians, though many will think
of death as the darkness below. One
or two may pray to enter it, tonight,
while there is still time to die all
at once in a great jellied ball of fire,
brief stars torn from their orbits. Landing,
the passengers scatter in all directions
and disappear into the city in cabs, on buses,
in subway cars. Some find someone waiting
and walk whispering arm in arm toward the car.
One man stands in the faint drizzle
and puts on his rain coat and hat. If he
hurries he can be home by dinner, and he
and his kids can watch television until

one by one they fall asleep before the set
and dream of those dark stretches that redeem
nothing at all or of the rain that hangs
above the city swollen with red particles
of burned air. One of them, perhaps the father,
may even dream of tears which must always fall
because water and salt were given
us at birth to make what we could of them,
and being what we are we chose love
and having found it we lost it over and over.

Three

Get Up

Morning wakens on time
in subfreezing New York City.
I don't want to get out,
thinks the nested sparrow,
I don't want to get out
of my bed, says my son,
but out in Greenwich Street
the trucks are grinding and honking
at United Parcel, and the voices
of loudspeakers command us all.
The woman downstairs turns
on the TV, and the smoke
of her first sweet joint rises
toward the infinite stopping
for the duration in my nostrils.
The taxpayers of hell are voting
today on the value of garbage,
the rivers are unfreezing
so that pure white swans may ride
upstream toward the secret source
of sweet waters, all the trains
are on time for the fun of it.
It is February of the year 1979
and my 52nd winter is turning
toward spring, toward cold rain
which gives way to warm rain
and beaten down grass. If I
were serious I would say I
take my stand on the edge
of the future tense and offer
my life, but in fact I stand
before a smudged bathroom mirror

toothbrush in hand and smile
at the puffed face smiling
back out of habit. Get up,
honey, I say, it could be worse,
it could be a lot worse,
it could be happening to you.

You Can Cry

I am in an empty house, and the wind
is blowing the eucalyptus so that the branches
sway slowly with a great sea sound,
and although it is dark, I know their movement
having seen it at dusk for years of summer
when the long day's last winds rose suddenly.
The five great branches lifted in soft light
and let their dusty leaves hold the moment
and then settled back with the long sigh
of an old man at that hour setting
down his tools. And I remember that man,
Old Cherry, his black head running with gray,
bowed in his bib overalls, letting the scarred
handle of the sledge hammer slide through
his thick fingers and burying his ashen face
in a red bandanna, twenty-eight years ago
beside a road long since dismantled
and hauled off in truck-loads of broken bits.
If he rose now from the earth of Michigan
where he rests in the streaming gowns
of his loss, Old Cherry Dorn, and walked
over the whole dark earth with one hand
stretched out to touch a single thing
he'd made in a lifetime, he would cross
this continent to where the last sea fills
the night and his one sigh is lost in sea sounds.
That is the sea, that is the moment that fills
my house with the wailing of all we've lost
until there is nothing left but dust falling
into dust, either in darkness or in the first
long rays of yellow light that are waiting
behind the eastern ranges. Do you hear

the moaning of those great lifting arms? That
is the sea of all our unshed tears, that is all
anyone can finally hear, so you can cry,
Cherry, you can cry forever and no one will know.

Above Jazz

"A friend tells me he has risen above
jazz. I leave him there . . . " Michael Harper

There is that music that the hammer
makes when it hits the nail squarely
and the wood opens with a sigh. There is
the music of the bones growing, of
teeth biting into bread, of the baker
making bread, slapping the dusted loaf
as though it were a breathing stone.
There has always been the music
of the stars, soundless and glittering
in the winter air, and the moon's
full song, loon-like and heard only
by someone far from home who glances
up to the southern sky for help and finds
the unfamiliar cross and for a moment
wonders if he or the heavens
have lost their way. Most perfect
is the music heard in sleep—the breath
suspends itself above the body, the soul
returns to the room having gone in dreams
to some far shore and entered water
only to rise and fall again and rise
a final time dressed in the rags of time
and made the long trip home to the body,
cast-off and senseless, because it is
the only instrument it has. Listen, stop
talking, stop breathing. That is music,
whatever you hear, even if it's
only the simple pulse, the tides
of blood tugging toward the heart

and back on the long voyage that must
always take them home. Even if you
hear nothing, the breathless earth
asleep, the oceans at last at rest,
the sun frozen before dawn and the peaks
of the eastern mountains upright, cold
and silent. All that you do not hear
and never can is music, and in the dark
creation dances around the single center
that would be listening if it could.

Making Soda Pop

The big driver said
he only fucked Jews. Eddie smiled
and folded his glasses
into their little blue
snap case and put the case
into his lunch bag. Last night
I think she was your sister.
This was noon
on the loading docks
at Mavis-Nu-Icy Bottling,
Eddie and I side by side
our backs to the wall,
our legs stretched out
before us the way children
do on a sofa. Ain't got
no sister, Eddie said.
Must have been
your mother then. Eddie
landed first
and the man, older and slower,
fell back out of the shade
into the cinders
of the rail yard. The guy
beside me went on chewing.
Eddie came slowly forward
crouching, his weak eyes
wide, and swung
again, again, and the man
went down heavier
this time and didn't
try to get up. Eddie
came back to his place

beside me, no smile on
his face, nothing, and opened
a peanut butter sandwich.
Alvin, the foreman, looked up
and said, OK, you guys,
this afternoon cream soda.

One

When I was only a child I carried
a little wooden sword in my belt
and with it I could face the dark,
I could descend the shaky steps
to the basement and there enter
each shadowed corner and even stare
at the thousand tearful eyes
of the coal bin. Later, still
a boy, I heard my brother crying
in his bed next to mine, not
for fear of the dark or because
the dead would not return or
for the dull ache of his growing.
In December of '51 on the night shift
a plain woman from West Virginia
began suddenly to curse this life.
She untied the rag that hid
her graying hair and wiped her face
and still the words came. "It's shit.
That's just what it is, shit." No one
answered or took her in his arms
or held her hand, and before long
she'd bowed her head to the wheel
that polished the new chromed tubes,
and all our hours passed a moment
at a time and disappeared somewhere
in the vast unchartered spaces between
the moons of our blood. Now if I
stood before myself naked in my body
flecked with graying hairs, I would cry
out that I too am still only a boy
and the great vein that climbs down

my shoulder and into my right hand
stumbles under the will of heaven.
I am burning in this new summer,
I am one with the scattered roses,
one with the moon waning long
before dawn, one with my brother
who has come down from the sky
and that long lost woman who told
the truth and received at daybreak
one toothless kiss on her forehead
from our father and mother the rain.

The Doctor of Starlight

"Show me the place." he said.
I removed my shirt and pointed
to a tiny star above my heart.
He leaned and listened. I could feel
his breath falling lightly, flattening
the hairs on my chest. He turned
me around, and his hands gently
plied my shoulder blades and then rose
to knead the twin columns forming
my neck. "You are an athlete?"
"No," I said, "I'm a working man."
"And you make?" he said. "I make
the glare for light bulbs." "Yes,
where would we be without them?"
"In the dark." I heard the starched
dress of the nurse behind me,
and then together they helped me
lie face up on his table, where blind
and helpless I thought of all
the men and women who had surrendered
and how little good it had done them.
The nurse took my right wrist
in both of her strong hands, and I
saw the doctor lean toward me,
a tiny chrome knife glinting in
one hand and tweezers in the other.
I could feel nothing, and then he said
proudly, "I have it!" and held up
the perfect little blue star, no
longer me and now bloodless. "And do
you know what we have under it?"
"No," I said. "Another perfect star."

I closed my eyes, but the lights
still swam before me in a sea
of golden fire. "What does it mean?"
"Mean?" he said, dabbing the place
with something cool and liquid,
and all the lights were blinking on
and off, or perhaps my eyes were
opening and closing. "Mean?" he said.
"It could mean this is who you are."

Steel

Foxtails, vines, black rocks, small streams,
thistles, and here and there a bright bird
leaping from branch to branch, and then
the whip bird uncoiling his wild song. We
climbed higher and higher through the dense
forest of eucalyptus until the sea broke
below and the bright golden shore curved
landward for a time and then jutted back
to hold the steel town of Woolongong
over which a brown scum rode. I thought,
This is just like home, and before me
flashed that distant Sunday afternoon
on which I waited at a railroad crossing
while the tanks, one to a car, their guns
dropped and frowning, passed for some
fifteen minutes, and I wondered how
many deaths they would contain and would
one be mine. It was my cousin, not I,
in Patton's army at a famous bridgehead.
His widow came to stay with us, still not
thirty, a silent woman, childless, asking
for nothing. Over thirty years ago,
and even here on a clear winter Sunday
at the other end of the world that life
intrudes asking still to be dealt with,
understood, accepted. Names I have lost,
faces with no more character than the moon,
swim up out of my life. Someone has found
a long vine, and we take turns swinging
out and back over a patch of rocks
and spikey bushes. I'm once again
a child on a children's outing. We will build

a small fire from fallen boughs and eat steak
and sausages and drink the soft dry wine,
and lie back in the late sun, dozing until
the first cold winds chill our brows.
At last the ocean darkening against
a low sky breaks cold and persistent over
the pocked stones, and we watch in silence
at dusk a herd of deer descending through
the fringe of forest to drink cautiously
at an old well. I could name these people
I will never see again, the mother and child,
the young painter full of hopes, the one
returned from Italy, his face creased
and tight as he bowed before a tiny thorn bush
and said its name over and over. Now I can hear
over the sea roar the great rolling mills
of Woolongong and the breaking of metal
on metal in the tides of the mind. I see
men and women stand back to let it happen, as
though the sea could stop, or steel, or memory.

I Remember Clifford

Wakening in a small room,
the walls high and blue, one high window
through which the morning enters,
I turn to the table beside me
painted a thick white. There instead
of a clock is a tumbler of water,
clear and cold, that wasn't there
last night. Someone quietly entered,
and now I see the white door
slightly ajar and around three sides
the light on fire. I remember once
twenty-seven years ago walking
the darkened streets
of my home town when up ahead
on Joy Road at the Bluebird of Happiness
I heard over the rumble of traffic
and the rumbling of my own head
for the first time the high clear trumpet
of Clifford Brown calling us all
to the dance he shared with us
such a short time. My heart quickened
and in my long coat, breathless
and stumbling, I ran
through the swirling snow
to the familiar sequined door
knowing it would open on something new.

Voyages

Pond snipe, bleached pine, rue weed, wart—
I walk by sedge and brown river rot
to where the old lake boats went daily out.
All the ships are gone, the gray wharf fallen
in upon itself. Even the channel's
grown over. Once we set sail here
for Bob-Lo, the Brewery Isles, Cleveland.
We would have gone as far as Niagara
or headed out to open sea if the Captain
said so, but the Captain drank. Blood-eyed
in the morning, coffee shaking in his hand,
he'd plead to be put ashore or drowned,
but no one heard. Enormous in his long coat,
Sinbad would take the helm and shout out
orders swiped from pirate movies. Once
we docked north of Vermillion to meet
a single spur of the old Ohio Western
and sat for days waiting for a train,
waiting for someone to claim the cargo
or give us anything to take back,
like the silver Cadillac roadster
it was rumored we had once freighted
by itself. The others went foraging
and left me with the Captain, locked up
in the head and sober. Two days passed,
I counted eighty tankers pulling
through the flat lake waters on their way,
I counted blackbirds gathering at dusk
in the low trees, clustered like bees.
I counted the hours from noon to noon
and got nowhere. At last the Captain slept.
I banked the fire, raised anchor, cast off,

and jumping ship left her drifting out
on the black bay. I walked seven miles
to the Interstate and caught a meat truck
heading west, and came to over beer,
hashbrowns, and fried eggs in a cafe
northwest of Omaha. I could write
how the radio spoke of war, how
the century was half its age, how
dark clouds gathered in the passes
up ahead, the dispossessed had clogged
the roads, but none the less I alone
made my way to the western waters,
a foreign ship, another life, and disappeared
from all I'd known. In fact I
come home every year, I walk the same streets
where I grew up, but now with my boys.
I settled down, just as you did, took
a degree in library sciences,
and got my present position with
the county. I'm supposed to believe
something ended. I'm supposed to be
dried up. I'm supposed to represent
a yearning, but I like it the way it is.
Not once has the ocean wind changed
and brought the taste of salt
over the coastal hills and through
the orchards to my back yard. Not once
have I wakened cold and scared
out of a dreamless sleep
into a dreamless life and cried
and cried out for what I left behind.

Those Were the Days

The sun came up before breakfast,
perfectly round and yellow, and we
dressed in the soft light and shook out
our long blond curls and waited
for Maid to brush them flat and place
the part just where it belonged.
We came down the carpeted stairs
one step at a time, in single file,
gleaming in our sailor suits, two
four year olds with unscratched knees
and scrubbed teeth. Breakfast came
on silver dishes with silver covers
and was set in table center, and Mother
handed out the portions of eggs
and bacon, toast and juice. We could
hear the ocean, not far off, and boats
firing up their engines, and the shouts
of couples in white on the tennis courts.
I thought, Yes, this is the beginning
of another summer, and it will go on
until the sun tires of us or the moon
rises in its place on a silvered dawn
and no one wakens. My brother flung
his fork on the polished wooden floor
and cried out, "My eggs are cold, cold!"
and turned his plate over. I laughed
out loud, and Mother slapped my face,
and when I cleared my eyes the table
was bare of even a simple white cloth,
and the steaming plates had vanished.
My brother said, "It's time," and we
struggled into our galoshes and snapped

them up, slumped into our pea coats,
one year older now and on our way
to the top through the freezing rains
of the end of November, lunch boxes
under our arms, tight fists pocketed,
out the door and down the front stoop,
heads bent low, tacking into the wind.

The Present

The day comes slowly in the railyard
behind the ice factory. It broods on
one cinder after another until each
glows like lead or the eye of a dog
possessed of no inner fire, the brown
and greasy pointer who raises his muzzle
a moment and sighing lets it thud
down on the loading dock. In no time
the day has crossed two sets of tracks,
a semi-trailer with no tractor, and crawled
down three stories of the bottling plant
at the end of the alley. It is now
less than five hours until mid-day
when nothing will be left in doubt,
each scrap of news, each banished carton,
each forgotten letter, its ink bled of lies,
will stare back at the one eye that sees
it all and never blinks. But for now
there is water settling in a clean glass
on the shelf beside the razor, the slap
of bare feet on the floor above. Soon
the scent of rivers borne across roof
after roof by winds without names,
the aroma of opened beds better left
closed, of mouths without teeth, of light
rustling among the mice droppings
at the back of a bin of potatoes.

—

The old man who sleeps among the cases
of empty bottles in a little nest of rags

and newspapers at the back of the plant
is not an old man. He is twenty years
younger than I am now putting this down
in permanent ink on a yellow legal pad
during a crisp morning in October.
When he fell from a high pallet, his sleeve
caught on a nail and spread his arms
like a figure out of myth. His head
tore open on a spear of wood, and he
swore in French. No, he didn't want
a doctor. He wanted toilet paper
and a drink, which were fetched. He used
the tiny bottle of whisky to straighten
out his eyes and the toilet paper to clean
his pants, fouled in the fall, and he did
both with seven teenage boys looking on
in wonder and fear. At last the blood
slowed and caked above his ear, and he
never once touched the wound. Instead,
in a voice no one could hear, he spoke
to himself, probably in French, and smoked
sitting back against a pallet, his legs
thrust out on the damp cement floor.

—

In his white coveralls, crisp and pressed,
Teddy the Polack told us a fat tit
would stop a toothache, two a headache.
He told it to anyone who asked, and grinned—
the small eyes watering at the corners—
as Alcibiades might have grinned
when at last he learned that love leads

even the body beloved to a moment
in the present when desire calms, the skin
glows, the soul takes the light of day,
even a working day in 1944.
For Baharozian at seventeen the present
was a gift. Seeing my ashen face,
the cold sweats starting, he seated me
in a corner of the boxcar and did
both our jobs, stacking the full cases
neatly row upon row and whistling
the songs of Kate Smith. In the bathroom
that night I posed naked before the mirror,
the new cross of hair staining my chest,
plunging to my groin. That was Wednesday,
for every Wednesday ended in darkness.

—

One of those teenage boys was my brother.
That night as we lay in bed, the lights
out, we spoke of Froggy, of how at first
we thought he would die and how little
he seemed to care as the blood rose to
fill and overflow his ear. Slowly
the long day came over us and our breath
quieted and eased at last, and we slept.
When I close my eyes now his bare legs
glow before me again, pure and lovely
in their perfect whiteness, the buttocks
dimpled and firm. I see again the rope
of his sex, unwrinkled, flushed and swaying,
the hard flat belly as he raises his shirt
to clean himself. He gazes at no one

or nothing, but seems instead to look off
into a darkness I hadn't seen, a pool
of shadow that forms before his eyes,
in my memory now as solid as onyx.

—

I began this poem in the present
because nothing is past. The ice factory,
the bottling plant, the cindered yard
all gave way to a low brick building
a block wide and windowless where they
designed gun mounts for personnel carriers
that never made it to Korea. My brother
rises early, and on clear days he walks
to the corner to have toast and coffee.
Seventeen winters have melted into an earth
of stone, bottle caps, and old iron to carry
off the hard remains of Froggy Frenchman
without a blessing or a stone to bear it.
A little spar of him the size of a finger,
pointed and speckled as though blood-flaked,
washed ashore from Lake Erie near Buffalo
before the rest slipped down the falls out
into the St. Lawrence. He could be at sea,
he could be part of an ocean, by now
he could even be home. This morning I
rose later than usual in a great house
full of sunlight, but I believe it came
down step by step on each wet sheet
of wooden siding before it crawled
from the ceiling and touched my pillow
to waken me. When I heave myself

out of this chair with a great groan of age
and stand shakily, the three mice still
in the wall. From across the lots
the wind brings voices I can't make out,
scraps of song or sea sounds, daylight
breaking into dust, the perfume of waiting
rain, of onions and potatoes frying.

Wisteria

The first purple wisteria
I recall from boyhood hung
on a wire outside the windows
of the breakfast room next door
at the home of Steve Pisaris.
I loved his tall, skinny daughter,
or so I thought, and I would wait
beside the back door, prostrate,
begging to be taken in. Perhaps
it was only the flowers of spring
with their sickening perfumes
that had infected me. When Steve
and Sophie and the three children
packed up and made the move west,
I went on spring after spring,
leaden with desire, half-asleep,
praying to die. Now I know
those prayers were answered.
That boy died, the brick houses
deepened and darkened with rain,
age, use, and finally closed
their eyes and dreamed the sleep
of California. I learned this
only today. Wakened early
in an empty house not lately
battered by storms, I looked
for nothing. On the surface
of the rain barrel, the paled,
shredded blossoms floated.

Then

A solitary apartment house, the last one
before the boulevard ends and a dusty road
winds its slow way out of town. On the third floor
through the dusty windows Karen beholds
the elegant couples walking arm in arm
in the public park. It is Saturday afternoon,
and she is waiting for a particular young man
whose name I cannot now recall, if name
he ever had. She runs the thumb of her left hand
across her finger tips and feels the little tags
of flesh the needle made that morning at work
and wonders if he will feel them. She loves her work,
the unspooling of the wide burgundy ribbons
that tumble across her lap, the delicate laces,
the heavy felts for winter, buried now that spring
is rising in the trees. She recalls a black hat
hidden in a deep drawer in the back of the shop.
She made it in February when the snows piled
as high as her waist, and the river stopped at noon,
and she thought she would die. She had tried it on,
a small, close-fitting cap, almost nothing,
pinned down at front and back. Her hair tumbled
out at the sides in dark rags. When she turned
it around, the black felt cupped her forehead
perfectly, the teal feathers trailing out behind,
twin cool jets of flame. Suddenly he is here.
As she goes to the door, the dark hat falls back
into the closed drawer of memory to wait
until the trees are bare and the days shut down
abruptly at five. They touch, cheek to cheek,
and only there, both bodies stiffly arched apart.
As she draws her white gloves on, she can smell

the heat rising from his heavy laundered shirt,
she can almost feel the weight of the iron
hissing across the collar. It's cool out, he says,
cooler than she thinks. There are tiny dots
of perspiration below his hairline. What a day
for strolling in the park! Refusing the chair
by the window, he seems to have no time,
as though this day were passing forever,
although it is barely after two of a late May
afternoon a whole year before the modern era.
Of course she'll take a jacket, she tells him,
of course she was planning to, and she opens her hands,
the fingers spread wide to indicate the enormity
of his folly, for she has on only a blouse,
protection against nothing. In the bedroom
she considers a hat, something dull and proper
as a rebuke, but shaking out her glowing hair
she decides against it. The jacket is there,
the arms spread out on the bed, the arms
of a dressed doll or a soldier at attention
or a boy modelling his first suit, my own arms
when at six I stood beside my sister waiting
to be photographed. She removes her gloves
to feel her balled left hand pass through the silk
of the lining, and then her right, fingers open.
As she buttons herself in, she watches
a slow wind moving through the planted fields
behind the building. She stops and stares.
What was that dark shape she saw a moment
trembling between the sheaves? The sky lowers,
the small fat cypresses by the fields' edge
part, and something is going. Is that the way
she too must take? The world blurs before her eyes

or her sight is failing. I cannot take her hand,
then or now, and lead her to a resting place
where our love matters. She stands frozen
before the twenty-third summer of her life,
someone I know, someone I will always know.

Four

The Harbor at Nevermind, 1915

The dawn is early. It was brought in
by four fishing boats that rowed back
on a calm sea with no catch at all.

The morning is angry. The little boats,
empty now, knock knock against the pier.
A wedge of burned coffee drives down

from the village, wakening slowly, one
house at a time where the fishermen
have gone back to bed nursing their rage.

If that were not my father standing
alone between two huge graying rocks
this could all be nothing or a dream.

If this were not the end of a year
at war, I could turn from the page
and go about my morning calmly

and you could amble to the window
seventy-eight years from here and gaze
into a cloudless sky for a sign.

Suddenly you take my hand and we
peer into the haze of our century
hoping to find an answer somewhere

in the great mushroom of imagery.
We find instead the rain driving down
on the ruined harbor, the houses closed,
the sea giving away less than it knows.

Ascension

Now I see the stars
are ready for me
and the light falls upon
my shoulders evenly,
so little light that even
the night birds can't see
me robed in black flame.
I am alone, rising
through clouds and the lights
of distant cities until
the earth turns its darker
side away, and I am ready
to meet my guardians
or speak again the first words
born in time. Instead,
it is like that dream
in which a friend leaves
and you wait, parked
by the side of the road
that leads home, until
you can feel your skin
wrinkling and your hair
grown long and tangling
in the winds, and still you
wait because you've waited
so long. Below, the earth
has turned to light but,
unlike the storied good
in Paradise, I see no going
and coming, none of the pain
I would have suffered had I
merely lived. At first
I can remember my wife,

the immense depth of her eyes
and her smooth brow in morning
light, the long lithe body
moving about her garden
day after day, at ease in the light
of those brutal summers. I can
see my youngest son again
moving with the slight swagger
of the carpenter hitching
up his belt of tools. I
can even remember the feel
of certain old shirts
against my back and shoulders
and how my arms ached
after a day of work. Then I
forget exhaustion, I forget
love, forget the need to
be a man, the need to
speak the truth, to close
my eyes and talk to someone
distant but surely listening.
Then I forget my own trees
at evening moving in the day's
last heat like the children
of the wind, I forget the hunger
for food, for belief, for love,
I forget the fear of death,
the fear of living forever,
I forget my brother, my name,
my own life. I have risen.
Somewhere I am a god.
Somewhere I am a holy
object. Somewhere I am.

Keep Talking

If it ain't simply this, what is it?
he wanted to know, and she answered,
"If it ain't just this it ain't nothing,"
and they turned off the light, locked
the door, and went downstairs and out
of the hotel and started looking around
for a bar that would stay open all night.
In the first one she said, "When do
you close?" The bartender said, "What's
yours?" Then he got mad, her man,
because she'd asked politely, and so
he shouted, "Please answer the question."
Then he said, "How late are you open?"
"Until the law says we gotta close."
They went out into the early summer
which was still light even though
kids were probably already in bed.
The wind stood out against the sails
on the Sound, and the last small boats
were coming in on the blackening waters.
After a while he said, "Maybe we could
just eat and take a long walk or sit
somewhere for a while and say things."
She didn't answer. The wind had picked
up and just might have blown his words
into nothing. "Why don't we talk?"
he said. She turned and stared right
into his eyes, which were light blue
and seemed to be bulging out with tears.
He was unshaven and wore a wool cap
which he'd removed. "I've been here
before," he said, "as a boy I wanted

to talk about things, but there was no
one to talk to." "Talk to me," she said.
"I don't know what to say. I didn't
know then." "When," she said. "When
I was a boy." So she explained that
being a kid was not knowing what to say
but that now he was a grown man. The lights
of the city were coming on, the high
ones in the tall buildings repeated
themselves in the still waters now as dark
as the night would ever be. He thought
about what she'd said and was sure
it had been different, that other kids
spoke about who they were or walked
with each other and said all the things
that jumbled in his head then and now.
He sat down on the curb and pressed
his face into his knees. She just stood
looking down at the shaven white back
of his neck, thin and childish, and she
thought, If it ain't this what is it?

Alba

The old North Station in Barcelona. Late Sunday night,
the last of the stragglers has stumbled in from the towns
down the coast, the pickpockets have gone off to stake
their women and kids to full meals at the American bistros
along the Gran Via. In one corner a tiny man hums
"I Can't Get Started" as he sweeps up the ticket stubs
into little gray hills. For a moment the lights
blink off, then blink on, he goes on humming and pushing,
pushing and humming, as though he'd mastered this work.
Let us assume he is an actor preparing for a role,
let us assume that before the night ends a woman will
enter the terminal and sit in one of the metal pews,
a woman this night draped in a blue dress, a woman
lacking a round hat, gloves, even the smallest suitcase,
someone from another movie. When the lights blink off
the woman cries out against her solitude, she is young,
too young to understand, and when the lights blink on
the little Andalusian is faithful to his part, although
the tune is now "The Man I Love" without the least
trace of irony. If I had a cigarette I would smoke,
if I had a bottle of cognac I would toast the lights
that have held steady for moments on end or my eyes—
behind glasses—opened in wonder, if I had a clue
as to why a week has come to this, I would rise above
the newspapers at my feet and proclaim in the name
of the Last Republic of Women and Men, my secret voice
echoing in the huge cavern until the old world ended.

This World

The murderers grew tired and rested under the trees,
no longer joking. Unseen, a west wind carried off
the smoke of their cigarettes. A brown wave crawled
shoreward, just a single wave, for the sea too
had wearied of its crests and troughs that gleamed
with the bodies of the drowned. My brother-in-law,
Petty Officer Casmirski—more handsome than Valentino,
my sister said—did not rise up from the depths,
his .45 holstered, his GI shoes gleaming, to spit
tobacco in the face of a god and pour great falls
of dark water from his eyes. In the same world
at dawn my grandmother's bus slipped into Los Angeles
unseen by the sun of paradise, and coatless she walked
the miles to her brother's house more determined than ever
to live in Christian Science and professional wrestling.
Early November, and already snow whitened the peaks
of the Sierras and eastward whirled around the stalled cars
on the Outer Drive and filtered through the little chinks
I'd stuffed with newspaper to melt on the floor
of my living room, one moment a diamond of hope,
the next a tiny puddle of filth. Four blocks away,
her sweater turned up over her thick forearms, sweating,
my great-aunt Tsipie leaned her whole weight into her labor
for that night's family feast and sang to her final child,
her dwarf daughter, her little Annie, who hummed back
as best she could. The strudel dough rolled finer and finer
as the hours passed and the old songs passed back and forth.
While the oven warmed, the earth turned its ear slowly
to hear these melodies come so many hard miles to fill
our mouths with water, flour, cinnamon, and black fruit.

The Letters

My friend Arnold wrote me how his life
changed the night he sat up in a car
speaking with a woman he'd met
while picking cherries. The woman
was unafraid of the future, she wanted
to live as much as Arnold, she had nothing
but the money she earned picking cherries.
Oregon in late June, the light hanging on
long past nine, the sky a radiant blue.
She reached one arm out of the car window
to gesture to the night sky as the stars
began to emerge. The car was her brother's.
The three of them would wander the whole
Northwest in search of work and settle for
an autumn outside Billings where Arnold
built fence and Bailey, the woman, waited
tables in a small cafe on the Crow reservation
taking crap from no one. Winter just behind.
They never waited for spring and the cloudless
great spread of sky and the fields running off
in all directions yellowed with clumps of broom,
they never bent to the wild orchids hidden
in grass or the spikes of phlox at the roadside.
They headed south and spent two nights trapped
by snow in a mountain pass. The brother
dropped out, not—perhaps—out of their lives
but out of the letters, and when they got
to west Texas there were only the two
crossing the bridge at Juarez to find
the bus to Guadalajara. The story gets fuzzy
just here. They sold wood sculptures weekends
while Bailey painted and Arnold wrote

his first stories. I could go back to search
out the letters, six in all I kept that arrived
within a few weeks probably twenty years ago
when Arnold and Bailey were living in Oakland
two blocks from the freeway. They'd married
so many years earlier they'd become one person
in my mind. I know I won't find the letters.
I know it hardly matters. In the dark
I can see Bailey's hand, dark itself, stained
by the juices of the sweet cherries, reaching
out to speak to the stars clustered above,
I can see the sky deepen and disappear before
the early dawn stills the two of them,
stunned by how much they've shared
in just this one night and with words only.

Another Song

Words go on travelling from voice
to voice while the phones are still
and the wires hum in the cold. Now
and then dark winter birds settle
slowly on the crossbars where, huddled,
they caw out their loneliness. Except
for them the March world is white
and barely alive. The train to Providence
moans somewhere near the end
of town, and the churning of metal
on metal from so many miles away
is only a high thin note trilling
the frozen air. Years ago I lived
not far from here, grown to fat
and austerity, a man who came
closely shaven to breakfast and ate
in silence and left punctually, alone,
for work. So it was I saw it all
and turned away to where snow
fell into snow and the wind spoke
in the incomprehensible syllable
of wind, and I could be anyone:
a man whose life lay open before him,
a book with no ending, a widow
bearing white carnations at dusk
to a hillside graveyard turned
to blank rubble, a cinder floating
down to earth and blinking slowly out,
too small to mean a thing, too tired
to even sigh. If life comes back,
as we were told it does, each time one
step closer to the edge of truth,

then I am ready for the dawn
that calls a sullen boy from sleep,
rubbing his eyes on a white window
and knowing none of it can last the day.

Going Back

I opened *War and Peace* to reread the scene
in which Natasha's younger brother Petya
falls in his first battle, and Denisov turns
from the boy's body to lean against a wattle fence.
In memory I heard a man so wracked the Cossacks
thought at first they heard the yelping of a dog.

Before I could locate the exact page I found
maple leaves I'd brought back from the East
in 1972, seven perfect blood red
pansies pressed for safekeeping, a dried thistle,
poppy or rose petals so dark and fragile
they glowed in the lamplight like shavings of oak.

Beneath them the author's words seemed frozen
in a common language no one understood.
"The cause of the delay was Natasha's skirt . . ."
Outside the sky darkened. By the open window
with David Ber I sat, with Yenkl, Tsipie,
Abraham, with all my lost, while the rain fell.

On the Language of Dust

Though the wallflower is fidelity in adversity,
The broken straw the spoiling of a contract,
The sparrow sweeps the streets, the wren proclaims.
The neat and humble broom, bindweed, docile rush,
The cup of kindness spill through open hands,
The polestar is lost or shattered on the grass.

White poppy, sleep, my bane and antidote.
Pitch pine, you think you think too much.
For benevolence I peeled the squat potato,
For bluntness gathered borage; the oat hummed back.
The simple barn owl slept above my lintel
While the weekday came, the pale bride of no one.

When the Northern Lights go out the larks collide
And lupine takes their blood voraciously.
Indian jasmine, I attach myself to you.
The cabbage thrives and profits in its season,
But not the swallowwort that cured my heartache,
Nor lemon in its zest, nor solitary lichen.

Without the seven stars, without the moon,
Without the sun-drenched winds, without my care,
Birds pass above into the space where no birds are.
Rose, deep red, give me your bashful shame,
White rose, I am unworthy of you, rose,
Dog, thornless, full-blown, white and red together,

Blasted rose placed over two buds, rose of war,
White rosebud of girlhood, cluster and musk,
Ragged robin of wit, single, burned, bleached.
The silent days are one. Rose of endings,
Calm me now, night-blooming cereus, nettle,
Bravery of oak leaf, wingless, talk to me, foxglove.

A NOTE ABOUT THE AUTHOR

Philip Levine was born in 1928 in Detroit and was formally educated there, at the public schools and at Wayne University. After a succession of industrial jobs he left the city for good and lived in various parts of the country before settling in Fresno, California, where he taught at the University until his retirement. He has received many awards for his books of poems including the Lenore Marshall Award, the National Book Critics Circle Award, the American Book Award, The National Book Award, and most recently the Pulitzer Prize for *The Simple Truth*.

This book was designed by Gary Young of Greenhouse Review Press, and by Felicia Rice of Moving Parts Press. Illustrations are from the *San Joaquin Series* by Gary Young. Thirty-five copies of this book were hand bound in a special edition by Timothy Geiger and Shari DeGraw, and were signed by the author.